D1711675

Candidreams:

I Remember the Beginning

Candidreams:

I Remember the Beginning

Candie Ferald

Little Girl Productions, LLC. Richmond, Va

Candidreams: I Remember the Beginning

Although spiritual in nature, this book contains mature subject matter that may not be suitable for children.

Dedicated to the Lost

♥

Inspired by the Faithful

To Ryan,
On behalf of your
loving mother Jackie,
aim high and shoot
for the stars.
God bless.
♥ Candie

Candie Ferald | 8

In Memory of my brother Taurean

I will always love you and miss you.

Table of Contents

Chapter 1:

Whose Child Am I?

1– Can-dling Instructions

I prefer being treated gently,
  although I can be rather hard.
It's because I hold in highest esteem
  that I am a creation of God–
Don't lessen me to a fixation,
  something to temporarily suit your cause.
Treat me like life means something–
  like you know that there is a God.

2– Focus

I remember the beginning...
  is the goal still the same?

If my vision has remained unchanged,
  then how did I get here, to this place,
  seemingly so far away from what I wanted,
  what I needed, my undeniable desires?

How did the road become cloudy?
So I relive...
  I drawback on former feelings–
  to build on the hopeful ones,
  learn from the discouraging ones.
There is so much to consider,
  that at times, I can't even see.

How quickly my view changed
  when I lost sight of the target,
I removed my eyes
  for what seemed but a second,

simply to notice other people
living their dreams.

.

Many times I was envious–
measuring others' struggles against my own.
I berated the Lord, "Why me?"
"Why" everything?"

Somewhere among all these questions,
I lost my focus...
the purpose of me traveling this road
in the first place.

3– Be Careful

Be careful what you see
   when you look at me.
I know you see what you like
   but do you see what you need?

I can't be less than honest
   to be truly Who I am.
I can't be less than free-
   to experience all I can.

I won't answer to any word
   or name that narrowly defines.
I can't live for anything,
   save the dreams of my mind.

And I surely can't live my life
   if not in pursuit of God's joy,
Therefore, I can't live my life
   with a man who is a boy.

Be careful what you see,
   moreover what you say or do.

Yes, I'm checking you out
  and it's God I'm looking through.

4– Amazing!

Tell the story of
  amazing things!

Like a fiery sun
  and a bird with wings,
  a rose's petals,
  a mighty oak's leaves,
  hands to write and
  lungs to breathe.

Doggies to pet and
  cookies to consume,
  the sweet personality
  of my very own room.

Toes that curl and
  cheeks that blush,
  who could have thought
  little things would mean so much?

A stereo blasting
  that stirs the feet

and the big block party
  that unites by beat.
A patient approach
  to fulfilling my needs and
  the faith of knowing
  Who resides in me.

Tell the story
  of amazing things!

Like a heart that loves
  and a mind that thinks,
  a spirit that grows
  and what it explores,
  enough that is abundant
  and requires no more.

A mouth with which to testify,
  the human body that you use,
  a glorious plan for your spirit
  found by exploring your truths.

Tell the story of amazing things!
Better yet, live it!

5- EXCUSE ME PLEASE!

EXCUSE me PLEASE!
I have my hopes and dreams,
  plenty of good things to do with my time
  that an uneventful imagination
  may never lead you to find.

Riches of knowledge,
  more than can ever be conceived,
  are readily available
  if just we believe
  and it seems by your actions, you don't.

Sooo, excuse me please,
  I've got dreams and
  plenty of fascinating things
  to do with my time–
Oceans to sail, mountains to climb,
  trees, LIFE, to plant and watch grow.
I need to fill the gaps of what I don't know.
I have souls to meet and answers to find.

My dreams have everything!

They are a cornerstone of my mind.
So, excuse me please, I have dreams!
You won't be wasting my time.

Don't take it personal.
I won't stand for your grief.
Move out of my way and loosen my feet.
There will be no barrier
  between my hopes and dreams and me.

So hear me the last
  cause I've said it already thrice-
Excuse me, PLEASE!
I've got my dreams but sadly...
  not enough time.

6– Soul Defying Frustration

What my soul needs
  to stay in stride,
  is the picture in my mind
  that won't intertwine with reality.

The thoughts are all mapped out
  with more doubt
  than confidence they'll actually work.

I got a fountain of ideas
  that I didn't ask for,
  but finally I learned to be grateful.

I wanted to be just normal.
That experience avoided me,...
  so very early, I had to learn
  how to love myself.

It's tough to draw the line,
  to precisely define
  personal success.

I try to discover,
 one way or the other,
 my best and optimum balance
 to maintain.

But life won't have it,
 I'm trapped just the same
 by my inability
 to fulfill my own dreams.

7– Spiritual Thirst

Constantly questioning,
  forever reaching,
  relentlessly searching,
  desperately seeking.

Am I a fool,
  to hunt for the truth?
If I see it, will I believe it?
If in front of me, will I achieve it?

There's nothing but energy
  as I seek the very things of my life,
  nothing but God.

I keep going,
  never knowing exactly
  when the pursuit shall end
  or when will I,
  or how much more
  should I even try.

I pray that my faith is enough,

even though I know it is nothing at all–
compared to what God has done for me,
to answer all my questions.

8- In Taurean's Light

It was a beautiful day for a wedding,
  one of the most special days indeed,
  but sadly this matrimony
  only exists in my dreams.

It is of my 18 year old brother,
  and such a good brother was he–
  his smile, his manner, his charm,
  numerous many things he led me to see.

The brightest day of his life,
  the proud, honored groom
  was shadowed by the truth,
  he was to die much too soon.

I was furious in my dream–
  trying to perfect the day
  but no one seemed to care.
They did what they wanted anyway.

I fumed and I shouted.
I stomped all over the place!

How could they take this so lightly–
   his last, important day?!

I was way pass fed up,
   just couldn't take anymore,
   then I noticed my brother laughing
   and harder than ever before.
.

I wondered what was so funny
   and how could he be so calm.
He said, "Sister, don't be angry,
   I'm just laughing at you in love.

Stop worrying over the ideal or
   fret not having your way.
Heaven lasts forever.
We can do this again someday."

9- Duality

Ambition and anger,
  I am a two-headed beast.
Grounded firmly and steadily–
  stretching ahead of me
  is a long and winding road,
  full of surprises,
  both good and bad,
  from which I callously choose.

I have nothing to lose
  but what I have not had at all.
What good is life if I don't fall?

Then I can't get up–
  the pleasure of rising again
  after falling so hard
  almost takes away the bitterness.

Almost...
  so I keep striving again,
  being weighed down
  by this two-headed beast that I am

but finding the energy and ability
to again plunge forward
and keep going,
though not knowing
for certain
my so-called sacrifice will pay off.

What will I show for my life?
Hardship and strife
   or peace and joy?
It is my choice
   and it is my right
   to claim what is for me!

So, angrily I survive,
   ambitiously I strive,
   being fueled
   by this two-headed beast that I am—
   wondering which will stand in the end.

No time nor need to worry now—
   my Master has a plan.

10- A Good Cry

All I required was a good cry.
I just needed to let some loose-
I had to let that sorrow go
   anger and frustration to diffuse.

I was knotted and saddened up,
  bent and miserable inside.
My heart knew nothing but grief,
  chaos had control of my mind.

The torment tortured my soul,
  crept into every nook of my being.
This suffering intent on destroying me
  left no other way of healing.

Even my spirit itself was aching,
  pleading for calm satisfaction
  and oh how those reins fell,
  this necessary human reaction.

Seemed I nearly let a river go
  to ease my bitterness and pain.

I almost cried my eyes out
    to feel like myself again.

I surely let it loose,
    released that anguish so hard–
    just me, myself and I,
    those four walls and my loving God.

I felt some agony was lessened
    as tears rolled off my shoulders.
How magnificent to have my Jesus
    to whom I turn my troubles over.

11- Bad Day Survival

What do you do
  when you have a day
  so bad to get through
  that you seriously doubt
  your dreams will come true.
For this day,
  it seems...
  you lack the mind, will or power,
  not even to mention
  the second, minutes or hours.

You feel yourself silly
  for thinking so high.
You feel yourself weak
  as tears mount in your eyes.

You feel yourself unworthy
  'cause you can't handle a task.
You feel yourself angry,
  wishing lost opportunity back.

You feel yourself selfish

for crying "Woe is me"
You feel so alone...
  convinced...
  you're the only one
  with your needs.

What do you do on those sad days–
  those incredibly bad days,
  those I can't wait until it's all over days?

Do what you should anyway dreamer,
  please continue to pray.

12- Whose Child Am I?

Maybe I'm my Papa's child,
  he's the only father I'll ever know—
  the man that fed me,
  gave me shelter and clothes,
  took me into his home
  and raised me as his own
  because I am his own.

He taught me how to be strong,
  to stand up and speak my mind,
  to not let the evils of the world blind me.
My beautiful Papa, with that fury such a flare—
Thank you. I got it too. All seekers beware.

I'm my Papa's child. This I know,
  because I handle my business—
  sunshine, rain, sleet and snow.

But maybe I'm my Grammy's child—
  I can be sweet you know,
  but as sweet as my Grammy,
  the extent can not be told.

My Grammy taught me compassion,
  to be kind, loyal and true–
  to give, give, give, even the life in you...
It's my Grammy whose beautiful smile
  often makes me sigh
  'cause it's so full of light
  and she keeps me wondering why...

They say the same of me too.
Grammy, my inner beauty,
  I proudly get from you.

But maybe I'm my Mama's child,
  another her have I become–
  to handle some of the worst of life
  yet remain standing tall.

"Deal with it baby"
  are the words that I hear
  when I'm most alone
  and I stand in fear.

When I need someone to listen
  or to just say hello,

I call up my Mama
  but she's hardly ever at home.
She's out there working it...
  like she taught me to.
You go there, Deborah!
I'm a bad bitch too.

Whose child am I?
Whose could I be?
I know I'm God's child
  because He gave me all three.

Chapter 2:

The Beginning of Darkness

1 - Candidreams

I'm not talking about average dreams
  made by average beings,
  made with undeveloped thoughts
  'cause so far in their life
  they haven't been seeing
  what God meant them to see.

I'm not talking about everyday dreams
  with everyday ends or everyday means,
  although they involve
  everyday people and everyday things.

I'm talking about...
  because I'm experiencing...
Dreams so encompassing
  I can hardly sleep at night
  and am constantly lost in them
  in both sun and moon light.

Dreams so right here,
  I can capture their taste.
Dreams so beckoning,

I can't turn away.

Dreams so absolute,
  no other options remain.
Dreams so powerful,
  they often lead my way.

Dreams so full of flavor,
  they have their own demands.
Dreams so purely joyful,
  they couldn't have come from man.

Dreams nurtured way down deep
  in my ambitious heart.
Dreams so spirit filled,
  they never seem to run out.

Dreams so soul changing,
  dreams so specifically planted–
  God never would have put them there
  without a path to catch them.

2- No Mediocre Love

I'm not interested in a mediocre love-
  an easily forgot about love,
  one that leaves me room to even think of another.
I prefer a love that is the only picture my heart utters.
I need to stop wondering
  what all the fuss is about.

No, I won't be satisfied with a mediocre love-
  one that I have to contemplate
  and add up all the signs
  to define its realness.

I desire a that love that is
  as true as God's existence,
  that grounds me in
  a deep sense of freedom-
  profound enough that
  from this love's foundation,
  I can experience more
  than I ever could alone.

I require a love that personifies

God's meaning of passion,
perpetuates selfless giving and
is a drive for understanding.

I won't settle for a love that dwindles
when the new is old and
little things become big.
I don't want the time that has passed
between us to be questioned.

I demand a love that reinvents itself-
that builds on the good
and overcomes the bad
and anticipates the road
that stretches ahead,
when anger is only a human thing
and doesn't compromise the essence
that combines these two wholes.

A love that grows
through faith's spiritual connection,
a love that elicits endless affections,
a love that loves also the imperfections.

No, I'm not interested in a mediocre love,
  one that I have to question
  and add up all the signs.

I want a love that is deep, powerful,
  and authentic,
  a love that is eternally mine,
  a love that is...
  God given and divine.

3- Funny Definitions

Brother, what defines a man for you–
   the guiding principles you aspire to?

How did you learn what you should be–
   a book, something you read, or maybe TV?
Is it something to you your father once said
   or does it come from some picture in your head?
Do you boys spur you to manly pursuits
   or does your women define that word for you?

Was it a dream, fleeing thought or such?
Did it come from nowhere
   and you can't explain what?

So once again…
Brother, what defines a man for you–
   the guiding principle you aspire to?

You call yourself a man,
   a word you thoughtlessly use.
Because before you can be a man,
   you must do what a man Will do.

You must become your own man.

Sister, what defines a woman for you–
  the guiding principles you aspire to?

Did your Mama tell you what a lady should be
  or do you follow ideals written for TV?
Was it a teacher or some friend from school
  or did suddenly a vision appear to you?
Did an old church lady one day catch you ear
  or is it an old love's words you continuously hear?

Is your current man controlling your thought
  or did it come from nowhere
  and you can't explain what?

So once again...
Sister, what defines a woman for you–
  the guiding principles you aspire to?

You want to be called a woman–
  you've been trying with all your might.
Yet you don't pursue your own purpose,
  your own value you consider so lightly.

Have you any answers
  to the questions of this poem
  or is your mind so unused
  that thinking is long gone?

In your haste, so quick to grow up,
  you've created a trap in which you're stuck.
From whence come these definitions.
  we adhere to and portray?
Is is too late to break free
  and find your own way?

Funny, how these definitions
  have worked to confuse us all.
No one even knows where they started from.
The things that distinguish men and women
  are not too difficult to find.
Ask God what kind of person you should be
  and then open up your mind.

4– Missing…Out

Some battles you can't win,
  some folks you can't win over.
Some beings you can't please,
  some will hate one way or the other.

Some will prize disappointment
  or point blaming fingers until the end.
Some prefer being an enemy
  and have no idea what is a friend.

Some don't care to capture,
  not even hold for a second–
  they rebel from that feeling,
  things that are a blessing.

Some prefer to fight forever
  and wage bitter war.
Some fill space with misery
  and happiness is a chore.

Some find comfort in depression
  'cause that's where they planted seeds.

Some would rather find any reason
  for a chance to disbelieve.

Some would rebut with a story.
Some defend by quoting statistics.
But only by following Jesus,
  will you discover what you are missing.

5– Inside to Out

And they say,
  my smile suggests I know
  something they don't.

They ask why I don't tell my secret.

I reply:
The answer is not one
  the ears can hear
  or something the eyes alone
  can catch a hold of.

It's something powerful in my soul.
Indeed, the workings of the Lord.

For there is no secret which I command.
I was just raised to comprehend
  that what lasts forever
  is what lies within.

6– The Beginning of Darkness

Do you know how it feels
  to want something so bad
  that not having it
  makes you depressed and sad?

Unfulfilled desires and ignored needs,
  craving so much you can't even see.
What happens to those
  whose dreams never fly?
Does all that's real
  and sincere in them die?

Death by denial, pain but no gain–
Is this how the lost earn their name?
As hatred builds and hope runs away.
  the light is gone but darkness remains.

7– All This Love to Give

I have all this love to give
  and I want to share it to with you
  but…

You are too selfish
  to graciously accept
  the unconditional love of another.
Your stance causes me to wonder…
  what if all that beauty and strength
  in you were finally set free?
Free from those memories and pains
  that bind you to that place.

I have all this love to give
  and I want to give it to you but…
  you are too empty to notice
  that the whole me only begins
  with the picture you see…
That like you,
  I am too complex a character
  to sum up in the mere words
  of the vocabulary.

That like you,
  I am God created
  and it takes time and patience
  to know and understand
  the real me.

I have all this love to give
  and I want to share it with you but…
  your insecurities wish to control me,
  to change me and suppress me
  into what you think
  you need to survive.
If this is your war, I won't pay the cost.
This is My life, my dreams won't be lost.
.

I have all this love to give
  and I want to share it with you but...
  you are too unsure.
Who is the real you?
You hide behind so many faces,
  your very own reflection seems strange.
And sadly, the beginning of your journey
  is still so far away.

I have all this love to give
  and I want to share it with you but…

loves' experiences have taught me better.

8- Infinite Possibilities

(There is a Failure to Define Me.n)

There is a Failure to Define Me.

Let them call me crazy
  if crazy allows me to be everything
  that my faith qualifies.
I seek places beyond my brief imagination.
Open your mind to gather God's wonders.

Let them call me crazy
  if crazy leads me to find happiness
  where others fail to look.
The weak seed cannot grow to potential
  without a different way to love it.
Experience God's boundless wisdom and mercy.

Let them call me crazy,
  if I get a little angry sometimes
  that my goals are reachable
  yet I have not attained them,
  that I don't measure up to my own worth,
  and I would rather die trying

than to live settling
for the world's offer.
Understand the absoluteness of God.

Let them call me crazy
  when they cannot comprehend this place
  that I have actualized–
  my own world,
  centered around God.
Thirsty I searched.
Undeniably, I found.
Fathom my testimony.

Let them call me crazy
  if crazy allows me to call on God
  endlessly and without shame,
  now more often to praise Him
  when I call His name.

God is the same
  in trouble and in joy.
And I AM justified.
Because of Him,
  explore my infinite possibilities.

9– First Things First

I love myself!
I'm enamored with myself–
  one of the best people I know!
Even when I can't stand myself,
  I still love me so!

Self absorbed a little,
  vain a little more,
  pride is easily evident,
  yet confidence sometimes a chore.

I can't offer love to anyone
  if I can't discern it first in me.
Self love should be priority,
  not heeded as conceit.

My faults are easily visible–
  I can name more than you,
  I still have to love myself
  regardless of what ensues.

If you don't cherish yourself

thoroughly enough
to savor the contents of this rhyme,
life presents opportunity to change.
This testimony is mine.

10– A Sinner's Prayer

God save me from myself.–
 that is my constant prayer
 as I dive deeper into myself,
 into the unaware,

Into the sea of those
 who don't know You,
 not because they can't
 but because they won't.

God, save me from myself
 as I dive deeper into myself...

Into this comforting sea of sin
 that eagerly awaits me,
 that deceitfully soothes me
 as I loom impatiently–
 waiting for you to answer me.

Did I miss your call–
 for me to come back home,
 because I was too busy trying

to make it on my own?

I know that you will spare me
   once again in this time of need
   that I have created
   out of my own human errors
   and own evil ways.

You are ALL merciful!
It is You who holds tomorrow.
So it is with the deepest of faith
   yet the saddest of all sorrow.
   that I call on You Lord, God
   to save me from myself...
   as I sin impatiently.

Chapter 3:

From Where I Stand

1– That Lucky Girl

The worst version of pain
  that punishes my heart–
  I'm in love with a man
  who's getting ready to start
  his life over with someone new.
He never gave me a chance
  though my love is true,
  strong, faithful, and precious.

He'd rather be with her
  despite my confessions
  and prayers to the Lord–
  asking Him why
  on this whole big earth,
  I'm in love with a guy
  who doesn't know my worth.

I can't get past it.
I can never deny.
The ocean can't hold
  the tears I've cried.

I've tried others
  to take his place.
Nothing changes,
  I still see his face.

Living a lifetime,
  without this man by my side,
  must be the worst kind of suffering,
  and there's nowhere left to hide.

It feels impossible and
  I still can't fathom-
  that all my love
  will never matter.

How can I survive
  or be the best me-
  knowing that lucky girl
  is getting all the love I need?

2– A New Season

As sure as the wind blows,
  so does the approach of a new era.
  a new season in my life in which I am.
Once again, I renew my spirit
  and redefine myself.

This is the evolution of the person
  I have become.

We all possess the same potential to grow
  under the nourishment and mercy of God's light.
I stand as a tree in this light
  and I experience the rush of His truth.
Joy and knowledge of this new blessing fill me
  and I hold to the foundation that grounds me.

Positive and negative outcomes
  can not be predicted in the midst of change.
Faith must be the constant to which I hold
  but my weak hands are numb from grasping.
I wonder what meaning
  this new suffering has for me–

this suffering that I have wrought
because God only offers joy.

Ironically, it is only because I suffer
  do I appreciate that joy.
And at times, I perpetuate
  my own cycle of unworthiness.
But with faith and prayer,
  a new season again approaches.

And once again...
  I renew my spirit
  and redefine myself.

3– My Deepest Anger

No thought provokes me more
  than the thought of all that blood
  pouring down from my mother's forehead.

So much that it looked like
  a dark, red, velvet sheet
  and it seemed to cover her whole body
  from her forehead to her feet,
  flowing down over her eyes
  which were frightened wide open
  when she realized.

That moment has been frozen in time,
  locked in my mind.

My mother's horror,
  the deepest anger I can understand–
  the flow of my mother's blood
  and the rim in the other's hand.

An old, nasty basketball rim
  that was swung at my mother in anger.

It all began in a conversation
　　that ended in surprising danger.

My mother had only been asking,
　　questioning her best friend why...
　　what had she done so terrible
　　to push her friend's fury so high.

Mom followed after her friend,
　　still questioning her why.
By the time I looked again,
　　blood was pouring over her eyes.

All I see is my mother,
　　that sheet of blood pouring down
　　from my Mom's forehead
　　all the way to the ground.

Her head was so swollen
　　as she lay in the hospital bed,
I wouldn't have known it was my mother
　　except for the ring on her hand.

The charges were not processed,
　　that's what the judge had ruled.

The assault on Mom meant nothing to them–
  regardless of what we could prove.

Frozen in time.
Locked in my mind.
My mom became a victim and
  I'll never forget that picture.

That is the deepest anger
  that I ever care to understand.

4- Addiction

I don't know what to do
  with the Lord's high.
He gives me no way to control them.
They are layered with
  unpredictable ups and downs.
I question how to process them...

But a high I can buy
  is a high I know
  I can conquer and maintain.
I've researched its moods.
I've studied its cycles.
Drugs fit a certain frame.

I'm too scared to try a life
  minus the controlled high.
How will I subdue this depression?
What will comfort me?
What will entertain me?
What will hear my darkest confessions?

How will I satisfy my needs' appetite

if there's no adequate replacement?
How can I overcome my fears
   if I have no extra means to face them?

I agree now that addiction
   is depression's disease,
   one that I sadly let
   take a hold of me.
I'll do whatever I must
   to one day again be free.

5– Thin

Two sides of a thin wall
  masking each other well.
I dwell on both
  and can hardly tell–

Which is me and
  which is my other self?
Which is the better?
Which is the less?

I am a fighter, a winner.
I will survive
  despite the circumstance.
But what is the real battle...
  to keep what I have
  instead of aiming for something else?

Distinct views of an identical picture,
  with my very own eyes,
  I can barely see the union.

Disgusted by the ease of
  a meaningless existence–
  I try to find my way to
  the actual me God created.
Which part of me do I set free?
Which part do I hold on to?

Learning to let go,
  a hard thing about faith.
The moment is a fragile amount of time
  and I can't seem to catch
  my own best moment
  with these clumsy hands of mine.

I just pray constantly to God
  that I hold my faith together
  so I will be more able
  to withstand life's pressures.

6- That Certain Feeling

Can't tell you what I think
  for you'd know how I feel.
I'd scare you away too fast
  before finding out if it's real.

These butterflies in my stomach,
  this dizziness in my head,
  this fluttering in my heart,
  understand that I'm afraid.

I could easily succumb to these feelings–
  for these feelings are so grand,
  like I'm soaring over the highest cloud
  with wings that won't ever land.

As if I see the most handsome rose
  surrounded by choking thorns,
  still emanating life and beauty,
  radiance being its norm.

As if I see the tallest tree

maintaining through furious winds,
like I'm in some hopeless place and
you're the light breaking in.

Don't mean to sound so romantic.
Me? I'm love's biggest skeptic…
but I can't deny your appeal,
not even this heart
so impenetrably sealed.

I fear exploring what could be there,
where all these feelings could lead–
don't want to tread on uncertain ground
that may cause my heart to bleed.

I'm scared of sharing further
all that I think and all I feel.
I know I'm fearful of trusting–
that, I'm certain, is for real.

7- Celibacy and Me

Trouble is as trouble does–
 for me, it's usually a dick.
How do I proclaim to know it all,
 yet become the fool so quick?

It's not from any old cock I fall apart.
I return only if I see fireworks and stars
 and my toes won't uncurl,
 and I can't stop trembling,
 when he touches my pearl.
My eyes open wide in disbelief–
 how can something so heavenly
 cause so much grief?

Mind blowing, leg kicking
 teeth chattering, hand clapping,
 sheet tugging, bed wetting,
 trouble forgetting sex!!

If only my relations were average,
 then maybe my issues would be too.
 but my love making is so spectacular,

you should see what I go through.

So…now in order to avoid love's woes,
  I'm gonna put sex in my past.
And this time I really mean it–
  this time celibacy will last.
Surely this must be punishment
  for all the fornication I've had.

8– The Present Cause

So they inquired of
  the recent uproar and
  it's present cause.
I said with no doubt,
  almost to a shout:

He asked me...
"How does it feel to be thirty?"
I said, "Who me?
Don't I still look good?"
He said, "Yes, M'am,
  beg your pardon if I could."

"How does it feel to be thirty?", I replied
  with a sudden twist
  and a sexy ass smile.

Age ain't the thing
  that determines my style.

I'm a real woman with
  many sides and even more dimensions.

To define me by my age,
   that defies my comprehension.

Besides, what is thirty?
What does it mean?
What is any number,
   without our agreeing?"
How does it feel to be thirty...
   he foolishly sought!
I said, "It feels so good to be me,
   I hadn't given it a thought!"

So they inquired again
   of my uproar
   and its present cause.

Oh, I almost forgot
   the real reason was...
   he forget to tell me
   how good I look for thirty!

9– Identifying Peace

No slumbering peace
  can I now find,
  circling the matters
  that contort my mind
  and lead it wayward
  from heart and health,
  presenting such confusion
  I can't identify myself.

Except in some small gestures
  that escape most critique,
  by some detail,
  God presents them unique.

Verily unmatched
  and one of a kind,
  state the matters
  encompassing my mind.

10- From Where I Stand

This poem is about me and the picture you see—
  the one you want to understand so desperately
  in your sorry crusade to conquer me.

War is mental and it requires a solid plan
You must first know your enemy
  and where they stand.
But know me, you can never do
  'cause you start from a point of contempt and untruth.
"Do I know myself?" should be your first attempt,
  but you'd rather hate me and all my merriment.

You question my joy when my life is low.
You marvel often at my continuous flow.
How do I keep ticking when the winder's stuck?
How do I keep going? How do I get up?

I see you watching me,
  wanting to know so ominously
  about this special being that I am.
Where do I end and where do I begin?
What is that certain thing that I have—

that's made me invincible to your plan?

I say real easy. It's God's hand.
I now have no worries or fears I can't stand
  because my faith is in God and not in man.

So don't be surprised when your efforts can't shake me,
  when you try with all your might but still can't break me.
I'm God's child and only to Him must I answer,
  so I try to shine light and give glory to my Master.

But you have tested and angered me
  time and time again,
It's only God's mercy that keeps you from your end.
If you've heard nothing of all I've said,
  let this little morsel stay in your head:

When you're plotting and planning and wanting my end,
  you've got all tricks and you're ready to spend
  all your time and efforts trying to displace me.
I'll simply call on God. He'll come and save me

.

This is the knowledge that makes me bold.
This is the truth that fills my soul.
So if you become a problem

and I need His hand above,
you better pray He gently fix you
with His mercy and His love.

Though you've started this war
and now wish it could change,
you still have a chance
to salvage your name.

Where do I get these ideas and
how do I call them fact?
It's because God once delivered me
from that hollow place you're at.

11- Three Steps

Trying to protect the good in me,
  I fail to control the anger.
So sad I struggle yet
  to grasp the balance.

Emotionally I was buried
  in the darkness
  of my own pity.
Guilty and alone,
  I've found a place
  where happiness makes sense
  but still isn't a natural way of life.

I breathe deeply.
I relax my mind
  and I pray.

I try to find the good me-
  the me that God created,
  the me that strives
  despite complexities elicited
  by the cruelties of the world.

I do not walk this journey alone.
I know that now
  because I experience life
  to understand those parts of myself
  I had hidden.

I was so afraid and so guarded
  that I cheated myself and
  no one knows how much but me.

I breathe deeply,
I relax my mind
  and I pray.

Good memories sprout–
  seeds buried for a later time
  so I can recall the purity of my childhood mind
  when I didn't know how deep
  sadness really is.

I reweigh my footsteps.
I reflect on the best in me.

I breathe deeply.

I relax my mind
and I pray.

Chapter 4:

Always

1– Line Crosser

I'm considering crossing the line–
  my friend is just that fine.
I love the way he makes me feel.
I'm overwhelmed by his sex appeal.

I'm moved by his style and charm.
I'd just loved to be wrapped in his arms.
We mostly have fabulous times.
I admire his excellent mind.

I like how he plays and works.
I like how he's manly yet flirts.
  so I'm thinking about crossing that line.

I dig what I know of him so far,
  almost scared to discover more–
Is this escalating feeling being reciprocated…
  this desire to romance and explore?

I'm thinking that he does like me,
  in that boy meets girl kind of way,
  but once it's already done,

can't change the events of the day.

But my friend is just that fine!
I think about him all the time
  and I think about the ways and how often
  I would blow his excellent mind...
  and I imagine ways our bodies would intertwine.

Of each other, we'd be partaking and dining,
  no reasons for complaining or whining
  but plenty of smiles and sun shining.

Oh, aren't friends divine?
I've got to keep this good one of mine,
So I'm going to take my time
  if I really want to cross that line!

2– Always

The problem is
  I don't love myself enough–
That's what doctors say to define
  people with issues like mine.
I try with all my might
  yet temptations succeed despite
  my valiant efforts to deny them.

The church people say
  I don't love God enough
  when I can't turn away
  from the devil's plot,
  so I avoid them in shame.
  separating our pain.

I seem a different sort than them.
God always answers their prayers.
I notice He responds to me
  though sometimes my blessings
  seem like vapor in a dark night–
  that dramatically and hauntingly,
  I gain my strength most often by fight.

But let it be, if this is my story...
  His people I'm obliged to tell–
  despite any pain, God is my guide.
My soul will do quite well.

I've tried living life
  every which way I sensed
  that might impart that missing joy.
I experience peace and harmony most often
  when I'm completely honest with my God.

Totally disorderly describes
  this path I choose to take
  but God blessed me with my heart..
Long ago, He forgave my mistakes.

Continue to bless my family Dear God and
  all who have expressed their love.
Regardless of anyone's doubt,
  You've always had control.

3- Heart of the Lesson

You once were there
  but now are gone.
Please my loving heart,
  please turn back on.
My actions are lurid,
  consequences are thick.
What once came natural
  has departed as quick.
According to vibe,
  was once how I grew.
Being out of touch with myself
  is quite brand new.

I could have lost you
  from all the drugs.
Maybe I lost you
  from lack of good love.
Maybe I never truly had you
  so I don't actually know the difference.
I hope this is merely a rest
  and that this break isn't serious.

In either case,
  you seem neither here or there.
If you're still beating,
  I hope you're reviving somewhere.
Maybe I gave the impression
  that I did not care.
Dear vulnerable heart,
  I promise to lessen your wear.

I won't burn you out
  by my rash of decisions
  that mostly leave me plunging
  outside of my own vision.

I finally discovered
  I could give more thought
  to what I put you through.
Please, sweet, loving heart,
  I'll learn to be good to you.

4– Chaos From the Core

I might be his offspring
  but I didn't spring off him.
World knows I'm better for it,
  being raised by Mr. C.
Mr. C was my mama's dad,
  the best upbringing I could ever have.

Forget my biology–
  it's not what matters most,
A good father instills
 and then cultivates hope.

Forget my biology?
Sometimes I wish I could.
Just because of my anger,
  I can't forget Uncle Solid
  and Uncle Smooth.

I would continue further–
  expression is my soul's relief
  but I hate to tell people things
  that would make them sick to believe.

Yes, I would love to tell you my story,
You'd understand my hurt,
 but I can't elaborate further
 'cause parasites sue over words.

5– The March From March 94

It was March 94
  when I learned the awful truth.
If you found out the same,
  how would you get through?

I met each morning's awakening
  with tears running down my cheeks.
I lived out every hour
with my spirit trembling and weak.

On the dean's list in school,
  with one year left in college,
  it was March 94,
  I gained another knowledge.

It was late one Saturday night,
  I went to my Aunt Sweetie's home.
She called up Auntie Raye
  and they whispered over the phone.

On the very next afternoon,
  Sweetie and I traveled across the water–

She was looking for her older sister
  who had something to tell me, her daughter.

I knew it would be devastating–
  I could feel it in my soul
  but only from my Mama's lips
  could I believe what I was told.

I had heard the whisperings,
  seen the evidence of October 93.
March 94, my mom confided:
  She was positive. She was HIV.

It was then a new disease,
  the stigma nasty and stale
  so I strengthened up all my walls...
  who could understand this hell?

I became a different person
  to grapple with the trauma.
I couldn't believe this was happening,
  this death diagnosis for Mama.

It was March 94 that
  my mind and spirit were rearranged.

I only now realize
  how deeply I'd been changed.

6– My Second Best Friend

A roach saved my life today.
I wandered on it as I was pining away,
  waiting so patiently but waiting so long
  (it seems) for the weed man to come home.

Marijuana, this is my poem made for you
  'cause of some of the shit you see me through.
My second breath every morning you take,
  my first and last thing when I am awake.

It seems so strange to love something this way,
  that I just love loving it is all I can say.
Wacky weed, you're my second best friend.
Smoke, smoke, smoke, I'll do to the end.

That beautiful herb
  that rises from the earth–
  the price I pay
  is way less than worth
  what you do for me,
  you heavenly seed.

Pretty Jane, you're God's creation.
You're only a plant
  but you've spurred a nation
  of great lovers and thinkers,
  people like me,
  who can envision more
  than what their eyes can see.

It makes me wonder…are you that tree–
  the one that started the world's misery?
And it makes me wonder, if waiting patiently
  made the difference between Adam, Eve and me.

God grows this to me, I truly believe.
It's my peacekeeper when my bomb's atick.
It's my stress reliever when I need a quick fix.
It creates a space where my words can go.
It lessens the wall that blocks my flow.

What a wonderful gift, this great marijuana–
  thinking about it makes me holler–
  that I feel so good and I get so high…
Why is this illegal? Why? Why? Why?

It's a conspiracy,
  a plan by the man –
  to keep you from me
  but still in his hand.
.

But what can part the two of us?
Only God's will,
  it's only Him I trust.
God will end it (or me)
  when I've had enough.

7– My Steady Beau

Some I can discard and disregard–
  sometimes I just want to play,
  so I select myself a boy toy
  who will let me have my way.

I turn from the serious,
  avoiding maturity's path–
I'm not looking for a life mate now,
  just some fun and laughs.

I don't want nothing deep.
I'm not ready to reopen my heart,
  just a little man attention–
  for me, that's enough of a start.

I just want to tap my toes in,
  not go fully underwater.
I have the right at this give time
  to define my best fitting borders.

Life has been hard so far.
I'm not ready to be in love.

I feel I've given enough of myself.
I am now my primary cause.

Some may have their own opinion
  about the kind of person I have been
  but I know what I deserve–
  that's all that matters in the end.

So let's keep the serious light,
  the relations hot and heavy.
Freedom must endure.
My dreams are my steady.

8– Tempo

My sister said, "You can't dance
  and what do you call that move?"
I replied, "It has no name,
  it's just my own natural groove.

I glide with the vibe that guides me,
  bounce to the count that gets inside me.
No directions needed
  when I'm in my own world.
The only thing that's normal
  is what's deemed so by this girl.

I can't always set the pace.
I can't always adjust the tone.
But the one thing in my charge
  is to keep dancing on!"

"Whatever", my sister laughed,
  "whatever that's supposed to mean.
I hope you're not doing that
  where anyone else can see."

"Let them get their giggles", I answered.
"Let them gain joy's pleasure–
  as long as I'm being me,
  life doesn't get any better.

I earned my best moves
  by rebelling against fads or pressure.
Self expression is a responsibility,
  an absolutely unique endeavor."

9– Even When

It may be too late
  to coast through heaven's gates...
  I might have to beg and plead
  but one thing is for certain,
  don't pull the curtains–
I'll get in because I believe.

I'm far from perfect
  and I sin each day.
God loves me still
  even when I've lost my way.

There is no person
  who is all bad
  and completely lacks joy.
God made us for a reason.
I'm so glad that I explore!

God has His hands on me–
  that has always remained.
Don't worry about my sins.
He knows them before they were made.

He'll make a way
  out of no way,
  the choir joyously sings.
It is written
  we shall be known
  by the fruits that we bring.

God brought forth the heavens
  and created an abundant the earth.
Death will come for all of us
  as sure as came our birth.
He provides us eternity,
  divided in human time.
He grants us free will
  and fuel for creative minds.

He supplies us with everything
  you know to exist–
  and the unknown,
  the sight to imagine it,

This is MY God and yours!
He is the author of this planet.
As sure as my faith guides me
  even when I don't understand it.

10- Heartstopper

The last time I smoked that shit
  was a silly attempt to forget
  the list of things that happened to me,
  that caused me to want not to believe,
  that caused me to want to give up hope,
  and ignore the call of my dreams.
I let all I cared for
  slide through life's seams.

It was an attempt to deny the pains
  overtaking my heart,
  an attempt to elicit more strength
  when mine had run out.

The rock made me an accomplice,
  pushed me to the edge of destruction.
It had me surrendering
  to the world's cheap seductions.

Those wootas and spliffs,
  they hardened my walls,
  and made seem a bed of roses

the darkness in which I crawled.

That made ambition seem
  a naive and foolish pursuit,
  that made seem normal
  the tragedies I'd live through.

It had me feeling, truly believing
  love was never meant to last,
  that in this earthly world,
  I was a useless outcast.

I used the rock as a block
  to mask my terrible sadness
  but its numbing affects
  only exacerbated my madness.

The last time I smoked that shit
  was only an attempt to forget,
  the list of things that happened to me
  that caused me to think...
  I had no reasons to breathe.

11- Confessions, Fair Warning

What can you do to me…
  about what I've said I've done?
Expect that I won't answer
  to any but that One.
And if you have a question
  to whom am I referring,
  the only One Who is capable
  of releasing me from my all burdens.

Can you walk on water
  or turn the same into wine?
Can you feed five thousand or
  make a seeing man out of one blind?
Can you put out demons…
  return them to their hole?
  be raised from the dead,
  after dying three days before?

I'm not talking the usual death,
  but what they did back in those days.
I'm talking of crucifixion–
  I'm referring to biblical pain!

Consider this fair warning,
  more admissions to be made soon.
I must let go of the past,
  so for the future there is room.

I only reveal so much
  so that others won't be afraid–
  to know His love in unconditional,
  despite the errors we have made.

My words are not a mistake
  or some self serving publicity tool.
I'm releasing some of my baggage.
I have some traveling to do.

12– My Papa Is A Diamond

My Papa lives forever.
Thank You Lord
  for being so loving and clever
  to put this man into my life,
  who taught me to lean on
  the forever righteous and
  to "build my hopes on things eternal".

Now, You have called him home...
  so with faith, we all must let go.
For You have a heavenly agenda
  for him now, then and forevermore.

He'll be chatting with one sister
  and dancing with another.
He'll be touring God's palace
  and laughing with his brothers.

He'll be reminiscing with old friends
  while making new acquaintances,
Sure wish I could see the smiles
  on his, his Mom, and Dad's faces.

He'll be tossing snowballs
  back and forth, he and Taurean.
They'll be little boys together this time
  with an eternity to explore and they'll
  talk about his enchantment of Grammy.
And oh, how easily I forget how I met him,
  he became a father and she a mother
  and they gave the world
  my mom, Sweetie, Raye and Jr. (that's brother).

My Papa is a diamond still
  but no longer is he in the rough.
He's basking eternally in paradise now–
He and Jesus, Face to face, one and One.

13- Enticing

You are wonderful and surprising,
  way pass what my enterprising
  young mind could have even begun
  to even think...
  to grasp at one time.

Wonderful and surprising,
You intimately designed it-
  this, my life, with just me in mind.
Did I mention You are kind?...

While wonderful and surprising,
  in that Your merciful ways
  are just part of what enticed me.

Kind, wonderful, and surprising...
I'd almost take it for granted
  that You are wise-
  except that both sets of my eyes
  experience more of You each day.
Wonderfully enterprising,
  kindly designing to entice me,

mercifully, You show Your bounty.
So many times...
You surprise me to remind me.

Alphabetical Index

Topical Index

Most of my work is definitely for mature audiences. Here is a quick reference guide of other relevant categories:

Family Friendly

(These pieces can be shared with the entire family and there shouldn't be any awkward moments.)

Secular

(While I obviously believe in, love and follow God, there are fellow human beings who do not. Here are pieces they may enjoy.)

Grown & Sexy

(Do not let your kids read this stuff
unless awkward moments are your thing.)

Short & Sweet

(For quicker bursts of inspiration or when you only have time for just a taste.)

Bonus Selections

from my next book

Role Reversal: Turn Pain Into Power

Smooth Move

We made love that very morning.
He kissed me as I dropped him off at work.
He said he'd see me later.
I had a plan to conquer the world.

I made that day a busy one.
Got part time work, cleaning tools and a loan.
I thought we were in agreement.
We were to build something of our own.

But quickly the tables turned
  and the respect I thought I'd earned,
  was lessened to absolutely nothing
  because his hateful words did I spurn.

He was using his words to hurt me,
  thought he knew how to make me cry.
He said he'd been holding something back,
  still don't know if it were true or a lie.

I shrugged off what he said,
  demanding I react in anger.

Never did such a smooth move
   result in such life threatening danger...

From the dining area to the kitchen,
   bounced liked a ball down the hall,
   all the way to the bathroom
   where the sink broke my fall
   and once again to the living room
   where my back was framed in the wall.
His choking hands then gained my breath
   until the Lord heard my muted call!

Narrowly, did I escape him...
   I could feel a part of me moving on
   but obviously I was meant to live,
   not meet death in this domestic storm.

That was almost ten years ago.
This is the first real thing
   about that day I've written.
Yes, it took me all that long
   just to remove the sting of being bitten.

The Nothingness

Giving up is incompatible with my faith.
I'd easily reject the notion of its existence except
  I see folks doing so all around me
  seems all the time.
I become confused.

Giving up is so beneath my realm of thinking,
  I had to look up the words to even write this piece.
When I did so, my stomach became full of disgust.
  I imagined burning my dictionary except that I need and
love it so.

Giving up is poles apart from anywhere I fancy myself.
It is absurd to a spiritually ambitious child of God
  who knows that He has plans for her,
Those plans were laid out and perfected
  even before the earth was warm.
All I have to do is show up and obey.

Allowing the option of giving up
  creates discord in my universe.
It has no place.

It is a spot of nothingness
  surrounded by an abundance of blessings
  the Lord is waiting to bestow upon me.
That spot must be obliterated.

Giving up doesn't apply to situations that are unnatural or
wrong in the first place.
  It does not apply to those things that are against God's will,
  those very things that our endurance and abilities are meant
  to change.

It is not the same as rearranging, resting, reevaluating,
  reconstructing or reconstituting.
It is unlike formulating a new route when the path is
  blocked.
It is unlike designing a new key when there is no other door
  to that particular goal.
It is not abandoning a mission that would otherwise lead you
  away from God's designs.
Giving up? It is bullshit and is different from anything I ever
  want to know.

Front Cover Artwork Information

The artwork on the cover of *Candidreams: I Remember the Beginning* coincides with the central theme...that as an adult, I reached a spiritually dark, emotionally desolate and physically destructive place in my life. This place was not reflective of my God given gifts and potential and certainly did not reflect how I was raised. I was so deep into my sadness and despair that I didn't even recognize myself. In order to heal, I needed to understand exactly what happened to me...how and when did this darkness overtake and change me. I remember my beginning and I revisit my childhood which had been so full of hopes, dreams and promise. Determined, I summon the strength and faith to begin my journey.

I believe that those first hopes and dreams we have as children are seeds planted by God and that when combined with the awesome gifts He grants us, will lead to the life He intended for us...one that far surpasses our brief imagination. Sadly, for many of us, something happens that changes us, that tells us that those are just silly dreams that we will never accomplish. Someone tells us that we're too this or we're too that. This not only changes the course of our lives, but as we internalize this negative feedback, we also become changed on the inside. Imagine how much more wonderful this world would be if everyone possessed the confidence and opportunity to pursue those God-planted dreams.

The front cover artwork was designed by Logical Logos.com.

35707142R00076

Made in the USA
Middletown, DE
12 October 2016